Everywoman's Travel Journal

1⊖
Ten Speed Press
Berkeley, California

Everywoman's Travel Journal

Adventure is my only reason for living.

ALEXANDRA DAVID-NEEL

Ten Speed Press
P.O. Box 7123
Berkeley, California 94707
www.tenspeed.com

A Kirsty Melville Book

Distributed in Australia by Simon and Schuster Australia, in Canada by Ten Speed Press Canada, in New Zealand by Tandem Press, in South Africa by Real Books, in Southeast Asia by Berkeley Books, and in the United Kingdom and Europe by Airlift Books.

Cover illustration and design: Kathy Warinner
Interior design: Victor Ichioka
Researcher: Joli Kornzweig

Printed in the United States of America

Telephone numbers and addresses are correct at the time of going to press and may be subject to subsequent alteration.

ISBN 0-89815-802-8

6 7 8 9 10 — 02 01 00 99

❧ CONTENTS ❧

❧ PERSONAL DATA ❧

Name .... KeR + Downey LTD Astrp

Address and phone ...jr.safaris @ swiftkenya.co

.... 254 - 2 - 552378 F

891692 P/F

Overseas address and phone ....

....

In case of emergency, please contact ....

....

....

Blood group ....

Special medical information ....

....

....

....

....

Religion ....

Passport number ....

Air ticket numbers ....

....

....

....

....

....

❧ PACKING CHECKLIST: THE ESSENTIALS ❧

(See first aid and toiletries checklist on page 9 and carry-on checklist on page 12.)

- ☐ adapter(s)/converter(s)
- ☐ alarm clock/watch
- ☐ bandanna
- ☐ binoculars
- ☐ camera/batteries/film
- ☐ clothesline
- ☐ credit cards
- ☐ drain stopper
- ☐ driver's license
- ☐ earplugs
- ☐ eyeshade
- ☐ flashlight
- ☐ glasses/contacts (spare)
- ☐ guidebooks
- ☐ hanger (inflatable)
- ☐ itineraries
- ☐ lock
- ☐ maps
- ☐ money belt
- ☐ passport (and photocopy)
- ☐ pen
- ☐ plastic bags
- ☐ prescriptions (eyeglass/medicines)
- ☐ safety pins
- ☐ sewing kit
- ☐ sleep sack
- ☐ string bag (for shopping/laundry)
- ☐ student I.D. card
- ☐ sunglasses
- ☐ swimsuit
- ☐ Swiss army knife
- ☐ traveler's checks
- ☐ travel iron
- ☐ umbrella
- ☐ walking shoes/hiking boots
- ☐ _____
- ☐ _____
- ☐ _____

Other things you may consider taking with you are: a small photo album or "talking book," to show people you meet where you come from and what your family and friends look like; inexpensive little gifts, e.g., stamps, chewing gum, picture postcards from home, to give to new acquaintances; and some of your business or calling cards.

In May a bit cooler than you think. Take

Dougs camera.

❧ Packing Tips ❧

She who travels lightest travels grubbiest.

ERMA BOMBECK

- Keep your color scheme simple.
- Set out everything you think you must bring—and eliminate half.
- Two or three bottoms and three or four tops should see you through almost every sitution.
- Fold up silk blouses and shirts in plastic bags to avoid wrinkles.
- Keep accessories to a bare minimum and do not bring good jewelry or other valuables.

adapted from Judith Gilford, *The Packing Book*

❧ Health Tips ❧

- No special vaccinations are usually needed for travel in Europe, North America, and much of the Pacific Rim. If you will be traveling elsewhere, check with the Center for Disease Control in Atlanta, which keeps the most up-do-date records of health conditions and required inoculations abroad. Call (404) 332-4559 or (404) 332-4555. Or order their annual report, "Health Information for International Travel," from the Government Printing Office, Washington, DC 20402. Then consult with your doctor regarding inoculations and other health precautions you should take before leaving.
- Also, The International Association for Medical Assistance to Travelers (IAMAT) has a chart of recommended immunizations for more than 200 countries, and an international directory of English-speaking doctors.

  In the US: 417 Center St, Lewiston, NY 14092
  (716) 754-4883

  In Canada: 40 Regal Rd, Guelph, Ont N1K 1B5
  (519) 836-0102
- Check your health insurance coverage: purchase additional travel coverage if necessary.

- Drink water only from factory-sealed bottles.
- If the water is questionable, then so is ice, fruits, vegetables, dishes, or cutlery.
- To purify water:

  Boil it.

  Use a portable microfilter, such as PUR.

  Iodine tablets or tincture (follow package directions and don't use if you are allergic or pregnant).

✥ First Aid and Toiletries Checklist ✥

- ☐ adhesive bandages
- ☐ antacid
- ☐ antihistamine
- ☐ aspirin/Tylenol
- ☐ calamine lotion
- ☐ comb/brush
- ☐ condoms/dental dams
- ☐ contact lens solution
- ☐ contraceptives
- ☐ dental floss
- ☐ deodorant
- ☐ diarrhea/indigestion remedies
- ☐ hair dryer
- ☐ insect repellent
- ☐ laundry soap
- ☐ laxative
- ☐ lip balm
- ☐ menstrual cramp remedy
- ☐ moleskin
- ☐ motion-sickness remedy
- ☐ nail clippers
- ☐ nail file
- ☐ prescription medicines
- ☐ razor
- ☐ shampoo
- ☐ shower sandals
- ☐ skin lotion
- ☐ soap
- ☐ sunscreen
- ☐ tampons/pads
- ☐ toilet paper
- ☐ toothbrush
- ☐ toothpaste
- ☐ towel/washcloth
- ☐ water purification tablets or filter
- ☐ _____
- ☐ _____
- ☐ _____

- Keep prescription medications in their original bottles.
- Pack copies of all prescriptions.
- Bring your doctor's phone, fax, and/or e-mail numbers.

❧ NATURAL REMEDIES FOR TRAVELERS ❧

Bladder infections	cranberry juice
Bruises or strained muscles	arnica salve
Cold or flu	echinacea
Diarrhea	mint tea; "pill curing" (Chinese herb combination); Wakefield Blackberry Root Tincture
Hangover	nux vomica; "pill curing" (Chinese herb combination)
Headache	nux vomica
Jet lag	"pill curing" (Chinese herb combination)
Menstrual cramps	lobelia tincture; dong quai
Mosquito repellent (topical)	chrysanthemum extract; citronella; lemon eucalyptus oil; pennyroyal
Mosquito repellent (take internally)	Vitamin B
Motion sickness	powdered ginger capsules
Poison ivy or oak	echinacea
Skin injury (burns, bug bites, rashes, cuts)	Califora Gel; echinacea salve
Stomach upset	chamomile
Stress	avena; chamomile; chrysanthemum; ginseng; passionflower
Sunburn	aloe vera; ching wan hung (Chinese herb); vitamin E
Yeast infections	acidophilus; citrus fruit; plain yogurt

adapted from Thalia Zepatos, *A Journey of One's Own*
and Dr. Barry Rose, *The Family Health Guide to Homeopathy*

❧ On the Plane ❧

[The transatlantic crossing was] so rough
that the only thing I could keep on my
stomach was the first mate.

DOROTHY PARKER

- Dress in layers. Cabin temperature can fluctuate quite a bit on long flights, not to mention differences in climate between your point of departure and your destination.

- Dress for comfort! Wear loose-fitting, wrinkle-resistant clothes, and comfortable shoes. Low air pressure in the cabin will make you swell a bit, and clothes and shoes that fit fine on the ground may be uncomfortable at 30,000 feet.

- Smoking is allowed on many international flights. If you are sensitive to smoke, make sure to reserve (and confirm at check-in) a seat far forward in the cabin, away from the smokers in the back.

- Drink a lot of water—about a cup or two for every hour in the air. Cabin air is very dry and will cause dehydration. Avoid caffeine and alcohol for the same reason.

- Move around. Walk up and down the aisles periodically; flex your feet; stretch your arms up over your head; roll your shoulders and neck. Massage and flex your feet and legs.

- Eat light both before and during a flight. If possible, bring along high carbohydrate, low-fat snacks. Carbohydrates will give you energy and help you sleep, but protein will just weigh you down in the low-pressure atmosphere of the cabin. If you have reserved a vegetarian, kosher, or other special meal for the flight, be sure to confirm your order at the check-in counter, and with the flight attendant as soon as you board.

- Sleep all you can before, during and after the flight. If you are flying across many time zones, try to book a flight that gets in at bedtime—this will help you beat jet lag.

adapted in part from Diana Fairechilde, *Jet Smart*

❧ CARRY-ON PACKING CHECKLIST ❧

Pack things that you will want to have access to just before, during, and immediately after your flight or journey:

- ☐ addresses
- ☐ airsickness remedy
- ☐ cash, including enough local currency for taxi or bus fare
- ☐ change of clothes/shoes/underwear
- ☐ contact lens case and solution
- ☐ credit cards and long distance calling card
- ☐ customs papers and receipts
- ☐ eyeshade
- ☐ guidebooks
- ☐ headache remedy
- ☐ itinerary
- ☐ journal
- ☐ lip balm
- ☐ makeup
- ☐ passport and visas
- ☐ pen
- ☐ playing cards
- ☐ portable CD or tape player, and CDs or tapes
- ☐ reading material
- ☐ snacks
- ☐ tickets
- ☐ toothbrush and toothpaste
- ☐ traveler's checks (most should be in a money belt)
- ☐ travel pillow
- ☐ umbrella
- ☐ _____
- ☐ _____
- ☐ _____

She can't keep much trash in a Mustang,
and that's what she likes. Travel light
Don't keep
what does not have immediate uses.

LOUISE ERDRICH

❧ ITINERARY ❦

*Writers and travelers are mesmerized alike
by knowing of their destinations.*   P. I

EUDORA WELTY

DATE ...... May 11 00

   Depart ...... S.V.

   Arrive ......

   Accommodations ......

DATE ......

   Depart ......

   Arrive ......

   Accommodations ......

DATE ...... May 13   Nairobi = Kenya

   Depart ...... c/o Robertson

   Arrive ......

   Accommodations ......

DATE ......

   Depart ......

   Arrive ......

   Accommodations ......

DATE ......

   Depart ......

   Arrive ......

   Accommodations ......

❦ ITINERARY ❦

Days 12-14 DATE ..... May 24-26

    Depart ..... MANSAI MARA RESV.

    Arrive ..... SERENSETI NAT PARK, Mara S

    Accommodations ..... LODGE

Day 15 DATE ..... May 27

    Depart (fly) Nairobi + airport after

    Arrive ~~Dinner~~ + Dinner Lunch with astrid 11.40p Leave

    Accommodations Kwaheri ya KUONANa "GOODBY for now"

DATE ....

    Depart ....

    Arrive May 28 Brussels arr 7pm

    Accommodations ....

DATE ....

    Depart May 29 Leave 11:15 AM Brussels to JFK

    Arrive S.L.C. arr 6:10

    Accommodations S.V. arr 10:59

DATE May 11th Thurs

    Depart 7AM S.V. - Kennedy 825 PM Depart

    Arrive 8:25th May 12th Brussels

    Accommodations ....

Day 1 DATE 13th Leave Brussels 1085 AM

    Depart Arr. 10:45 pm Nairobi

    Arrive ....

    Accommodations "MacUSHLa House"

❧ ITINERARY ❧

DATE .... 14 – 16

Day 2 – 4

Depart .... Nanyuki to (Fly) to

Arrive ...... Shaba game Resv. + Uaso Nyiro Riv

Accommodations .... + Lorian Swamp
Tented camp

5 – 6 DATE .... 17 – 18 (fly to)

Depart .... chalbi Desert – N. Kenya

Arrive .. to see Kalacha Dida

Accommodations .... Eight bedded lodge

DATE ... cont. ...... Kalacha + Hurri Hills

Depart .. (fly to) Koobi Fora on Lake
Turkana

Arrive .... + Allia Bay + Sibiloi Nat Pk
+ South Island

Accommodations ...... See above

7 – 8 DATE .... 19 – 20

Depart .... fly to Mweiga then

Arrive ...... Aberdares Mt + Salient

Accommodations .... Tented camp

9 – 10 DATE .... 21 – 22

Depart .... Down to Rift Valley

Arrive ...... Lake Nakuru Nat. Pk.

Accommodations .. Tented camp

Day 11 DATE .... 23 ...... Fly To Rusinga Is
Lodge

Depart ...... Maasai Mara
Lake Victoria

Arrive ......

Accommodations .. Lodge

· 15 ·

Notes

Notes

Shop - Ann Cusic

THE URBAN Leopard

~~Kirby~~ Road General Mathenge "Masingeh"

WESTLAND   Tel 749 462

Notes

❧ RECORD OF TRAVELER'S CHECKS ❧ AND CREDIT CARDS

Lost or Stolen Traveler's Checks

Dial Collect from Anywhere in the World

American Express (801) 964-6665 • Citicorp (800) 645-6556
(813) 623-1709 • Mastercard International/Thomas Cook
(609) 987-7300 • Visa (410) 581-7931

From within the U.S.

American Express (800) 221-7282 • Citicorp (800) 645-6556
Mastercard International/Thomas Cook • (800) 223-7373
Visa (800) VISA-911

Number	Amount	Date and Place Cashed	Exchange Rate

❧ Record of Traveler's Checks ❧ and Credit Cards

Number	Amount	Date and Place Cashed	Exchange Rate

CREDIT CARD NUMBERS ....

....

....

Lost or Stolen Credit Cards

Dial Collect from Anywhere in the World
American Express (910) 333-3211 • Mastercard
(314) 275-6690 • Visa (410) 581-7931
From within the U.S.
American Express (800) 528-4800 • Mastercard (800) 247-4623
• Visa(800) 428-1858

❦ Record of Expenses ❦

Keeping a record of expenses will help with budgeting as you travel and with customs when you get home. For complete customs rules, send for a free government booklet:

> USA: *Know Before You Go*
> US Customs Services Office
> PO Box 7407, Washington, DC 20024

> Canada: *I Declare / Je déclare*
> Revenue Canada Customs and Excise Department
> Communications Branch
> Mackenzie Ave, Ottawa, Ont K1A 0L5

Item	Amount	Date and Place	Method of Payment

❧ RECORD OF EXPENSES ❧

Item	Amount	Date and Place	Method of Payment

❧ PHOTO RECORD ❧

Roll #	Dates	Locations

❧ ADDRESSES ❧

NAME . . . .

    Address . . . .

    . . . .

    Telephone . . . .

NAME . . . .

    Address . . . .

    . . . .

    Telephone . . . .

NAME . . . .

    Address . . . .

    . . . .

    Telephone . . . .

NAME . . . .

    Address . . . .

    . . . .

    Telephone . . . .

NAME . . . .

    Address . . . .

    . . . .

    Telephone . . . .

NAME . . . .

    Address . . . .

    . . . .

    Telephone . . . .

❧ ADDRESSES ❧

NAME ....

Address ....

....

Telephone ....

NAME ....

Address ....

....

Telephone ....

NAME ....

Address ....

....

Telephone ....

NAME ....

Address ....

....

Telephone ....

NAME ....

Address ....

....

Telephone ....

NAME ....

Address ....

....

Telephone ....

❧ Addresses ❧

NAME ....

    Address ....

    ....

    Telephone ....

NAME ....

    Address ....

    ....

    Telephone ....

NAME ....

    Address ....

    ....

    Telephone ....

NAME ....

    Address ....

    ....

    Telephone ....

NAME ....

    Address ....

    ....

    Telephone ....

NAME ....

    Address ....

    ....

    Telephone ....

❧ Addresses ❧

Name ....

    Address ....

    ....

    Telephone ....

Name ....

    Address ....

    ....

    Telephone ....

Name ....

    Address ....

    ....

    Telephone ....

Name ....

    Address ....

    ....

    Telephone ....

Name ....

    Address ....

    ....

    Telephone ....

Name ....

    Address ....

    ....

    Telephone ....

🌿 ADDRESSES 🌿

NAME . . . .

    Address . . . .

    . . . .

    Telephone . . . .

NAME . . . .

    Address . . . .

    . . . .

    Telephone . . . .

NAME . . . .

    Address . . . .

    . . . .

    Telephone . . . .

NAME . . . .

    Address . . . .

    . . . .

    Telephone . . . .

NAME . . . .

    Address . . . .

    . . . .

    Telephone . . . .

NAME . . . .

    Address . . . .

    . . . .

    Telephone . . . .

DATE ....

PLACE ....

DATE ....

PLACE ....

DATE Thurs May 11 2000
PLACE S.V. to Brussels

As Always Coop sets alarm wit 30
min to leave house. I wait and
wait. We are last people at airport.
650 for 7 AM flgt. But business class
makes up for it. Now leaving
Newfoundland for Europe, Time: 8:55 pm
Just finished Dinner. Will try my

What is more beautiful than a road?
new Dr type GEORGE SAND sleeping pill
in an hr and we'll sss. Worked!

Went to Sleep about 1015 and awoke
for breakfast about 7 our time.
May 12 Slept most of the time. Also
taking "jet no lag". We'll see
again.
         Get t nice Sleraton hotel
after customs and all 11 AM
Coop reads a bit then asleep
'til 3. I got an hour sleep
in. Then off to Central Brussels by
the train about 15 min. Walked around

DATE .... May 12 ..... cont: Fri
PLACE .... Brussels

in the rain. One nice arcade.
   Back to hotel about 6:45
Coop (naps sleeps) 8pm.   Interesting
Indian Dinner — a special
+ only at Sheraton.

Macushla
House

Another alarm clock awakening.
I imagine everyone in
africa is up early to see
the see the animals so best
get used to it. Would be
fine if we DIDN'T Go TO bed
at 11:45 always. Great breakfast
at the Sheraton

Plane left 1¾ hrs late
8 hrs flying time, plus 1 hr
stop some place near Entebbe.
A long trip. Couldn't Do it
without bus. class. Very comphy
seats. To bed at 1230

Breakfast 8 ish at Macushla
House. compy. Slept pretty
well — up at 310 am woke
at 710 and good breakfast

Flew over Nairobi
N for an hour to camp →
site

DATE ....

PLACE ....

DATE ..... Mar 14 .... Sun ....
PLACE ..... Leave Macushla House ..... for

camp site at Shaba N.P.
Quite a set up - at least
8 in help.

2pm Lunch at camp then
4:15 Walk - Saw Lion tracks
very recent + Elephant from
previous eve. Dik Dik, Impala,

> *It's rather nice to think of oneself as a*   Genewek
> *sailor bending over the map of one's mind*   grossbeok
> *and deciding where to go and how to go.*   3 dou
>
> KATHERINE MANSFIELD   3 guiea hens

Drinks 7pm by fire pit built by
the   Dinner
boys. 11:15 bed   with very early
awakening. So didn't take
sleeping pill so didn't sleep
after 3:10 awakening, same
as last nite, but did get
back to sleep abit. So
Thur Fr Sat Sun with No
Normal sleep, but feel almost
o.k.

DATE Mon Mar 15
PLACE Tent at ~~Shaba Res.~~ Isiolo
Roberbom own camp.

awakened at: 6 AM to go
seek Elephant which we
found after an hrs Drive,
a herd of 20-25. Then
breakfast in the veldt.
Took 6 guys with us. omelet
etc.

    Back to camp at NOON.
Lunch at 2.

    Weather great, sunny
hot, No too hot + cools
about midnight.

    At 4 off to see Edward's
Il Nangonya lodge built by
natives for whites.
    Supper 830 by the
fire in front.

DATE ....

PLACE ....

DATE .... Tues (I guess) ....

PLACE .... AT Shaba Reserve

awakened to
Up at 6 AM — to start early.
Slept last night til 530 — so
Getting better (with sleeping pill)
    Off to tour Lewa Downs
Privately owned 6,000 acre
ranch Emma + Will Craig.
Stop in for tea. Lots

We were very tired, we were very merry—
We had gone back and forth all night on the ferry.

EDNA ST. VINCENT MILLAY

of game in Lewa Down
  Drove out at 5pm Home
at 730.
        Local blk conservany
people at 7 pm. Two guys.
at Dinner at 9 to
bed at 10:50 ... 2only.

                     Lots
   not bad tent, loads of servue
from 90 mm and to sleeping
pill at work.

DATE ....

PLACE ....

awoken
Up 620 - breakfast - flew (20
                                flgt
with above to above, his
"resort"   STOPPED EN
route to see some
camel herders with
their sheep. Out in
nowhere in the dessert, just
a wee bit of dirty H_2O,
a spring, to attrack them.
Stopped again to explore
some high wall.
            Lunch at "the resort"
with natives, camels Ibis sleep
right outside the open Din Rm.
Saw all sorts of animals
away from anything. Flew
in very low.
            No Hot H_2O - was a
heater wash H_2O at Shaba
but here with have a

flush toilet - The stink
two people can make
in a "toilet tent" is
unbelievable. Makes you
feel Downright anamalistic.

5 pm Long Long walk +
rock climb wit James
and Jaime came to get us.
Nice setting under (moon) moon
for Dinner.

Left the boys in
the pool. Early again
tomorrow so to warm bed
(warm!) at 10:30

DATE .... Thurs 18

PLACE .... Kalachi   2ᴰ Day

(AM Flight)

Up early to fly N. To
Lake Turkana - about ½ way up
r Koobi Flora
on Rt side of lake. Leaky's
camp where oldest remains for
"Homo Habilis" were found. ½
mill yrs old. Pre Homo Erektis

> We all ended up somewhere with our
> various uncertain lives flapping about us
> in tatters and our pockets full
> of foreign coins.

KAREN ELIZABETH GORDON

Lunch at TITε camp after
1½ walk over the Digs.
(DIP)
Then a swim in the
Lake fly back to
"Roberts Ranch" for
Dinner and Dancing
Gabbra. Try to help
Coop with his video 😐 and

·43·

fly neTTing. He is very
happy. Talks to James
+ Jaime Roberts Ceaselessly
        Funny how well
one ADapTs To No
electricity tho ice is
tantamount on my desire
Flush toilets great.

approaching 1 wk.
Back to tents... o.k.
except stinking ecrement.

8 o'clock flight (improve
ment!) To the Cebadare N.P.
no [Meiwega then into the
Salient] Private entry
only 4 camp sites 6,000
acres. Flew low over
the Mts then into Nanyuku
where Jaime lives. Bonny
flew us abadares trucked
into camp. A walk +
lunch. Were up high,
a grassy knoll with forest
all around. The park is
fertile rich brown soil - lots
of little farms.
        All different birds
here. All Kenya birds have

triple barrel names. Impossible
to remember.

The "crew" all met
us smiling + hand shaking.
430 Drove all around
part of the park. Saw loads
of Cape Buffalo and
quick a few elephants +
3 or 4 bush buck.

Cool at night. first
nite without sleeping pill - Not
too bad.

DATE ..... May 20 ..... SAT .....
PLACE ..... Abadare N.P. ..... camp in the Salient
+ The Rift
Drove out at 6:30. We're Valley
wakened a 5:40 AM! OFF
to see 3 water falls - Drive
around the 60 sq mile Park. 4,600
Acres
off to the Highlands, high
"Moorlands"
very green.
Back for lunch at 3 pm

Never a ship sails out of the bay
But carries my heart as a stowaway. NOT me, tho
this trip Not
ROSELLE MERCER MONTGOMERY b.o

out Again at 5 pm to Do another
couple of routes, looking for
the elusive leopard. It's a
thing with James. Only saw
a baby hyena.

DATE ....

PLACE ....

DATE May 21 Sun
PLACE Lake Nakuru N.P.
Tents   bottom (S) of the End of the
                                        Rift Valley

Up 545 Again : awful. Drive
to Lake Nakura. Stop at the
Rift Valley cricket Club for a
drink while James + Tari
shop too for camp.

            Then tour around camp
looking for leopard +
everything else. A bit
tiresome really, but Coop
having a ball + James
also. I'd like to look at
a well lit bath + fridge.
            Picnic lunch is the
wild with zebra strolling
by.

            Out again at 430 for
usual game looking drive.
Saw elephant up close
AM + 1 leopard + lions
plus all the rest PM.

· 49 ·

Coop goes fast asleep at
1030. No time to read
or write all Day except
at 1030.

DATE ..... May 22   Mon
PLACE ..... Lake   Nacuru

Awake 5:45 ... really rather
awful. At This hr frigging
cold. But warms up nicely
During the day as, knock
on wood, it has been
sunny everyday. By getting

> It was like seeing the earth for the
> first time, and I felt less homeless there
> than I had ever felt anywhere. I feel very
> homeless.
>
> SARA WHEELER, IN CHILE

up early saw a pride
of lions with their kill.
A few buses in here. First
seen. Saw all the other
antilope, and lots of birds.
Every raptor here is an
eagle and the most
colorful birds are the
starlings.
          Came back to breakfast
at 11ish. Seemed like 4ish.

·51·

forget to write up yest pm
oh know its STILL TODAY.
Hard to imagine the length
of a DAY when you are
in the bush at 6:30 AM.

A long rest period
today, 1st so far.

Back out after 200
lunch at 245 to go
to the Lake Naharu, to
See Flamingos +
huge pelicans and drive
around seeing the rest.

Another good Dinner.
Food is good - very!

Another sunny DAY.

DATE Tues 29

PLACE Resnga Island Lodge
~~Resnga~~ Resinga

Goody goody breakfast at
7 fly out at 8, but still
awoken at 5:45, so breakfast
at 6:30. James thinks its
all a joke... so be it.

Arrive at this marvelous
flush toilet, lighting on a
generator lush spot but
immediately out on a flishing tired!
boat til 230!! Caught
5 perch. Coop one at 13 lbs!

Then a marvelous
big hot lunch. 45 min
to enjoy the spot we are
at. Very comfortable and
back out on the boat.

Thought at last I
could wash my hair but no
sense if on the boat.

Lots of exotic birds.
chirping and calling all the
time.

·53·

we are lucky to be here
off season. Opens June 1st
as Did Luwa Downs.
The lake sounds
like the seashore but no
beach.
Willie and Sue Roberts
(Not here) as Emma + Will
and Jaine Roberts all in the
"hotel" bus. Good for them.
Electricity is a
great invention only appreciated
when you don't have it.

DATE WED 24

PLACE Resianga + sister in law with Roberto
+ Mara Caro

Slept 'til M am in our
gorgeous surrounding and
comfortable bed, elec lights
from generator, big shower
etc etc. Late breakfast
walk with Philimon to see
the oldest skull in the world,

*It's easier to find a traveling companion
than to get rid of one.* I'm sure!

PEG BRACKEN

Mary Leakeys. Glorious
weather, good food, no bugs
anywhere! And very green.

3 pm flew to Masaii
Mara. Picked up " guide
dé Mattai plus 2 other Masai
Drove around saw the
usual plus hippo, lots of
hartebeast, topi, Masai giraffe - see
list.

Coop puts light out every
night at 10:30. why couldn't
he do that at home???
Also right after our 830 dinner.

·55·

Rain 6pm — 10pm
1st time!!
last time in
the WILD
at least.

DATE ..... Thur 25
PLACE ..... The Mara 2D Day

UP AT 545 again — Drove
around seeing Hartebeest
etc   ect. above chased
by Hyena, 40 hippo, 16
lions in a pride. Hot
sunny breakfast in the
veldt, ole Hattai, Tar and
us. Back to camp by
12:30 and lunch not Til
230.   2 whole free
hrs. Longest free time
since we left. Lots of
elephant.
      4 pm out for Cheetah
2D Day. None, but x the pride
of lions and 6 cubs all
playing together —
      Another great Dinner!
Parfiterols for dessert. Last
nite van. ice cream choc
sauce!!!

DATE ....

PLACE ....

Rain 7pm

DATE   The Mara (39)

PLACE   Fri 26   3º Day

Rise at 5:45   out to find
Cheet. 630 - 230 —   Saw elep. hippo
                              ete and
          Lunch   chicken curry   the pride

      4 -7 off for cheetah again.
No cheetah but lots of
crocks, elephant family, and
Lion mother + cub.

I questioned the luxury we have as
Westerners to pop in and out of
other people's lives.   Me too!

NAOMI ROBERTS, IN GHANA

The "last supper"
will   be   good.
        I can read a real
book   tonite,   nothing about africa!
Hah Hah — The cheetah hunt began
tomorrow on the way to the airport

Looked around at game
after 6:30 😊 awakening.
Plane left 10:00 for
Nairobi.

Met by Astrid + Emily
and drove to Marusla Lodge
to cleanup and have lunch
with PAM. Very civilized
place - sitting by the pool
writing this. Electricity and
all that. Really relaxing.
During During the trip thought
of Mr Cooper + Haley and how
much they would like — Tho the
children would to esp. D/S.

This has been a good
trip. Pampered by 8 in crew
and a few nice spots to
stay. Not much for camping
tho. And just as easy to see
game in a zoo, unless something
interesting happens between the

animals. After all the preserves are
just big zoos, but the changing
scenery is great.

Lunch at Macushla
by the pool!

3 -. Giraffe zoo, gift
shop, and baby animal
zoo to see tiny elephants
+ Rhino.

Back at 7 to
change for flight +
Dinner Macushla with Astrid
and Emily + Pam.

930 To airport
power outage so very slow
+ quite warm, Arr 1030
for 1130 flqt. Due to airport
power shortage no runway
ligts. Plane left at 3 Am
They kept us in a hot
stuffy lounge 3½ hrs. Pretty
miserable.

DATE Sun 28
PLACE Brussels arr 11:05

Rain just as Brussels was when we arrive!

Thank god for a Sheraton hotel. Most luxurious – so good to have thrown this extra nite in.

Will have 2ᴰ Shower wash hair – only been 14 Days – but really looks good, behaved well – No way to wash it.

Men travel faster now, but I do not know if they go to better things. Prob. NoT.

WILLA CATHER

lunch at the airport buffet AND off To the Hist. Military Museum, closed Due to a marathon of 2,000. To another historical spot closed Due to Sun, so back to hotel Sish. Went to "fitness center" and ross a bike for awhile, and then a quiet reaD. Was going to copy business

· 63 ·

DATE ....

PLACE ....

address book this trip but
No way.

Dinner in hotel. The
end is in sight. Pray
that tomorrows flight better
than todays. again, thank
You for the layover

A cold Beer pre Dinner!
:)

Good Dinner - nice
surroundings.   A good
Sheraton.

Up at 730 630 Narobi
time - where my "time-clock"
is now regulated. Will
try the homeopathic "No lags"
again. Didn't work going, for
sure.

Nice flist time 11:15 AM.
What Do I find at home??
Not home 'til 11 pm.

Now Brussels time
midnight and an hr more
to S.h.C then good wait
for connection to S.V.
Couldn't possibly Do This
except bus. class.

Guess i'll have to
write up the trip with
pics + map for Coop.

DATE ....

PLACE ....

SAMANTHA Baby 11 OCT 1c

MATTEUS Thayer   Anite Poley

Crystal Herbert

Tmp 23%

8 hr later there

Trem + ?

To PRAGUE

DATE Sept 26 Tues

PLACE BtR 800 678 1147   Kelly McCurrey

ANDrew SUSAN Drazen   Aspen
Barry amy Gordon
Piere Andrea Rinaro   onterio
Sheydon Mc Cinley   SAn DieGo
John Wall   MADison wi

VAn braght   Holman   Matiessen

Klinpel

*Generally speaking, women in the bush
tend to adopt the conventional female roles
…[i]t is considered unladylike for a
woman to swear and by the same token,
it really isn't on to swear in front of
a "lady."*

NERYS LLOYD-PIERCE, IN AUSTRALIA

DATE 26ʰ Tues Ⓓ

PLACE Hailey

Depart 944
" Cinn 618 arrive
Dep " 715 p.m.
Arr. Gatwick 730 Am

NOT so awful This time.
Did sleep a bit - one McCleam
pill. Very Sroggy A.M. but
not up all night.
    Then an awful bus - hot
crowded to Heathrow for our
cleck.
        Coop looses wallet on
the way. Arrive 2 hrs pre
depart so no place to leave
baggage and a long wait.
Weather great so far. Got
most of business work Done.
Nothing more I can De now.

    He hasn't heard one word I
    or the stewardess have said.

·68·

DATE ....27th, WED (WED) ②
PLACE ......Casa Marcello

Arr London 8 AM   Not Too bAD as
I Said   2 or 3 hrs sleep. Then
an awful bus to Air Clezz
at Heathrow, sort of, you
have to check in 3 hrs
early!!   So good we had
hrs to spare. At airport
845 til 3 o'clock Depart.
Hotel 4 star O.K.

8 pm waiting for Coop to wake
So we can eat. Tried to call
Klinsel who was due yest.
told not here til tomorrow
Now we have to sit in
the confines of this little
hotel to have his drinks.
could be worse — he DiDNT
watch TV.

    Dinner Casa Marcello.
Not BAD pasta. Too Tired to be
hungry. Bed by 1130 whee!

DATE ...... 29 ... Thurs ....
PLACE .... Casa .. Marcella...

Slept til Hammering
started.. just like Vienna.
so up 730 ish. Good pound cake
breakfast. Off to find Georges
hotel, leave note, + Am. Exp. re
Coops lost card. Then after
loosing him twice, let him
stay in front.. it works!!, we
saw the rulové castle. (Falling
asleep right now. Walked over the
charles Bridge. Home by
5:15!! ☺ Including a
good river side lunch.
          930 pm off to "The Red
Wheel" around the corner for
a quiet Dinner.
          Coop stops reading
at 12:15 😊

DATE ..... 30 Fri.

PLACE ..... Casa Marcello + Hoffmeister Hotel Stekel Hotel to meet.

up via alarm 6:45 A.M. :-) The Group collects at another hotel at 8:15 Hoffmeister, take bus awhile later to "Hotel Stekl" o.k. not special

Do 43 k after long barely o.k. lunch. Easy No hills, but bikes are

It's not good to take sentimental journeys.
You see the differences instead of the samenesses.

MARY ASTOR

heavy and couldn't get out of granny gear. Could be worse. Good weather and beautiful country

Dinner here o.k. Did get coop to bed by 11:45. I was exhausted.

Slept til 9. So
we missed the group
and biked with Coop,
as of yesterday. Not
good. Constantly argue
about DIRECTIONS. I
mixed up R/L twice(!).
But Coop was wrong
lots more. Coop fell of bike
at end of day - falling
on sand. Very mad at
me. Says he was waiting
for me to pass him. Crock
of bull.

Dinner at a winery
in Budjovick. ok meal
nice atmosphere.

DATE .... Sun ....
PLACE ....

    Was to tired to write.
73 K some good hills
        Lunch
    Dinner   on 'our own'
with the Holmes   good
but stomach not so good
        Great Scenery..

Rainy a.m. waited 'til
ten. turned into Decent Day
Quit hilly ride Great
countryside. Rode with Carol
+ Gene.

Dinner w/ "Monks Place"
Castleville USA Food N.A.T.
So hot

So tired - more tomorrow.
Don't know 'why.

Took bus from the Rutz hotel
in chec to Richard Lowenherz
(Lion hearted) in Durnstein
Austria. Best hotel so far: But one
bed
A well lit baTH! Some took
a short ride — was to be the
usual 43K, but DiDn'T sTop
raining Til after lunch. I

*If you travel far enough, one day you will
recognize yourself coming down the road to
meet yourself. And you will say YES.*

MARION WOODMAN

OpTED to come to hotel +
coop rode. Just O.K.

    ouT To "Backen" Restaurant.
Very posh. Everyone looked nice
Dressed up. The Peleton
V.B, Lt, Matt all quickly saT
togetter once again. Food
excellent just can'T eat
much. Don'T really feel well.
What's new .75. when travelling.

*/ / A little
/ /*

DATE .... WED ....
PLACE ....

Bike up + Down the
Danube Lunch In
Melk with all the
Jews? Pretty ride, tho
gloomy.

Very festive farewell
Dinner at the "Lowenhart."

Woke up 4 Am
with awful Diarrie.

only christian
at a table
of 7.

Great Sun.

DATE .... Thurs 5

PLACE .... Durnstein — Vienna

Took bus to Vienna
930 A.M. Sun came out
on the way.
    Hotel Kaiserin Elizabeth.
Seems very nice. Couldn't
get into "Koenig von Ungelt"
    Coop naps on
arrival. Our anniversary
430 !!! Dinner with Holman to
                            celebrate.
    Off to try to find
the good italian restaurant, for Dinner,
am. exp., + obviously lots
more historical stuff. ← No
had a nice lunch — which all
came right out and ran into
the whole bike group shopping
and Coop had to get back
to Am Exp by 5 so not
too bad.

· 77 ·

Vienna pretty civilized
after the last week.
Still crowded 'tho.

London ! Civilization
again. So good to
"home" again. Arrived
about 130 pm — unpacked
in a funky little rm. The
"Executive Hotel" is gone
as such, a wild modern spot
now. No place to hang anything,
No tub.

Off to Harrods for a
hair-cut wildly expensive
Kathleen did a terrible job
before I left. To get a
pocket book + hair stuff as it
was blown dry — $ .Down the
drain.

5pm Coop having his daily
nap.

Finally off78. to the Tail
+ swallow for Dinner — good!! Coops
neck in a brace from biking.

DATE .... SAT 7
PLACE^{Hotel} 57 Pont

All fairys around waiting
on you - but friendly. Breakfast
served on a tray in the bar.
      I went to the New
Tate, coop shopping, what else?!
The " was a disappointment -
more like a cold train station,
no feeling of a former power
plant. The new bridge was
closed.
  (x)

I was advised to dab malt whisky behind my
ears if I wanted to catch a MacDonald man.   It was

SARAH DALE, IN SCOTLAND

Packed — The two restaurant humongus
line. Huge line at 230 at Peter
Jones - Street packed with umbrella
topped people. The Sloane ST
      restaurant closed
Trading co big late lunch line.
Walked up to Brompton Rd packed.
Finally found lunch at "Gloriana"
French pastry place on Brompton -
last table at 3.30!
    coops Naptime starts at 8pm
again....

            Beccho Fino "for Dinner
                       good!

DATE .... Sun 8 ....
PLACE ....

leisurly morn for a
change — out To Seven
Oaks area (30 min train) to
"Ingthim Mote" — a smallish
house but nice — Quite
old went Thru many
owners — last one who
Donated it to National
Trust was John Robinson's uncle.
He stays there from time
to Time.

Back to town about
6:30.   Weather was
perfect.

It Dion't nap so
to Monza restaurant at
830 Excellent Dinner

Pouring

Off To Cleval Place
about 1130 - Unpack etc.
Nice to be "home", and
to sleep tonite in a
tucked in bed. No more
Duvets. My own rm even!!
        Went to the
Museum of London redone
all. Very well Done. Took
Coop exactly an hr
to Do first Rm. In
two 1/2 hrs standing almost
still saw 1/10 of it so
have to go back.
        Tried to find Holmans
apt for drinks at 6 pm.
Got totally lost couldn't find
it. Came out of serrch soaking
wet.   To Dinner Brasserie
st Quentin with Mobleys at
7:15. Still pouring. Good
Restaurant.

·81·

DATE ...... Tues 10 ......
PLACE ...... Cleval ......

COLD WINDY
then warmed
UP &
Some
SUN
then
//
//
//

Great sleep. No snoring.
Quiet breakfast in.

Back to Museum of
London — look at some stuff
again progress a few yrs
in 2½ hrs. Impossible to
really believe how long he
takes per exhibit case.

Then lunch at The National
Portrait Gallery and the
Tudor exhibit of painting.
It wasn't too big a
show thank God! Great
view from 4th Floor restaurant.

Crossley Cooke by
730 for Drinks

To the old Brays
for Dinner. All seems well
with Them and David was quite
well behaved.

grey, then
sun, then
/ / /
/ /

DATE ...... Wed 11 ....
PLACE ...... Cheval ....

off 1058 to Venetia
to Cookham Stanley Spencer
gallery, Then lunch chez
her + then Fawley
House — . a polish home,
Not Too big — rains
came just as we left.

Travelling alone is not lonely; it's an
extremely powerful feeling, very similar
to love—it's that kind of strength.

CHRISTINA DODWELL

Maidenhead is lovely
country.
                To Tail + Swallow
Fairholt St.

· 83 ·

DATE .... Thurs 12 ....

PLACE .... Clever ....

well, this is it - back
to normalicy soon, And lots
of bus. problem. My only
DAy alone - DiD a few
museums + researcled "our
area hotels"

To Dinner with
Babar Kimber -t Brasserie
SAN Quentin. good but not
hungry again.

DATE .... Fri 13 ....

PLACE .... Travel ... 19hrs flight Time, 22 Door to Door

leave cleval   8 20 AM

flight from Gatwick O.K.

So much better in the DAYtime.

8.30. Then get to S.L.C. the

430 is cancelled ~ on a 7:10

in at 11pm instead of 730pm.

So glad to be home

1. People seen   Venetia

Crosley. Cook

Barbara Kimber

and the unfriendly bike group

from S.V.   except the

Holmans.

Heath

I had diarrea for 4 Days

then at the end got

a runny nose HEAD COLD

and gave it to Coop

for last two DAYs.

I lost 4 lbs.

STILL SICK 16 Days Later
·but about cureD.

Places stayed:
Hotel Marek Prague
can't remember
Exec Suite - New 57 Pont
Cleval Place

DATE ....

PLACE ....

....

....

....

....

....

....

....

*The key to getting past their cautious shell
is to make the first move.*

STACY GILBERT, IN THE CZECH REPUBLIC

....

....

....

....

....

....

....

....

....

DATE ....

PLACE ....

*There are only two rules. One is E.M.
Forster's guide to Alexandria: the best way to
know Alexandria is to wander aimlessly.
The second is from the Psalms: grin like a dog
and run about through the city.*

JAN MORRIS

DATE ....

PLACE ....

DATE ....

PLACE ....

DATE ....

PLACE ....

DATE ....

PLACE ....

As a visitor, I am accorded the status of
honorary man and sit with them to eat.
A woman waits on us silently.

CHRIS JOHNSON, IN CHAD

DATE ....

PLACE ....

DATE ....
PLACE ....

*Too often travel, instead of broadening the
mind, merely lengthens the conversation.*

ELIZABETH DREW

DATE ....

PLACE ....

DATE ....

PLACE ....

....

....

....

....

....

....

....

Travel is the most private of pleasures.
There is no greater bore than the travel bore.
We do not in the least want to hear what he
has seen in Hong-Kong.

VITA SACKVILLE-WEST

....

....

....

....

....

....

....

....

....

DATE ....

PLACE ....

DATE ....

PLACE ....

....

....

....

....

....

....

....

*I attempted nearly everything at least once,
including great land snails, though I did
baulk at roasted bat.*

NAOMI ROBERTS, IN GHANA

....

....

....

....

....

....

....

....

....

DATE ....

PLACE ....

DATE ....

PLACE ....

DATE ....

PLACE ....

DATE ....

PLACE ....

....

....

....

....

....

....

*It is...the first time that I have really
examined my Western preconceptions. I
arrived expecting a war-ravaged, oppressed
land full of dying people, and discovered
that my image was years out of date.*

ANNA BORZELLO, IN UGANDA

....

....

....

....

....

....

....

....

....

DATE ....

PLACE ....

DATE ....

PLACE ....

....

....

....

....

....

....

I flatter myself I have already improved considerably by my travels. First, I can swallow gruel soup, egg soup, and all manner of soups, without making faces much. Secondly, I can pretty well live without tea.

ANNA LETITIA BARBAULD

....

....

....

....

....

....

....

....

DATE ....

PLACE ....

....

....

....

....

....

....

....

*As I passed a window, a young woman with
a glowing tan and confident gaze stared back
at me. I was looking in a mirror.*

MADELEINE CARY, IN THAILAND

....

....

....

....

....

....

....

....

....

....

DATE ....
PLACE ....

DATE ....

PLACE ....

....

....

....

....

....

....

....

It was a delightful visit—perfect,
in being much too short.

JANE AUSTEN

....

....

....

....

....

....

....

....

....

....

DATE ....

PLACE ....

DATE ....

PLACE ....

*I have before seen other countries, in the
same manner, give themselves to you when
you are about to leave them.*

ISAK DINESEN

DATE ....
PLACE ....

❧ SECURITY TIPS ❧

If you think you are too small to be effective,
you have never been in bed
with a mosquito.

BETTE REESE

- Travel light.
- Insure your belongings.
- Always keep an eye on your luggage, and lock it up.
- Carry all your valuables and important documents in a security wallet at all times.
- Keep photocopies of all important documents in a separate bag from the documents themselves—and leave a copy at home with a friend.
- Keep separate records of all your traveler's checks, and carry checks and large sums of cash in a security wallet.
- In crowds, carry purses, cameras, and day-packs in front of your body, and hold on to them securely.
- Lock rental cars and hotel rooms; keep your possessions out of sight.
- If you are traveling in a culture that is very different from your own, do a little advance reading on what behavior is culturally acceptable. When you arrive, look around: take behavioral cues from the people around you—how do they interact?
- Learn a few basic self-defense moves.
- Above all, rely on your intuition and instincts.

adapted from Thalia Zepatos, *A Journey of One's Own*

❧ TIPPING, BODY LANGUAGE, AND ❧ OTHER POINTS OF ETIQUETTE

*Travellers who require that every nation
should resemble their native country,
had better stay at home.*

MARY WOLLSTONECRAFT

- Arab countries: if you openly admire a host's possession, he will feel obliged to give it to you.
- China: avoid wearing blue and white—they are mourning colors.
- Colombia: it is impolite to yawn in public.
- Fiji: folded arms are considered disrespectful.
- Germany and Brazil: the American "okay" sign, with index finger and thumb forming a circle, is an obscene gesture.
- Ghana: do not gesture with your left hand.
- Greece and Bulgaria: a head nod means "no."
- Iceland: tips are considered insulting.
- Mexico and Latin America: tips are solicited for just about any service. Ask a local friend, or the concierge in your hotel, what is considered appropriate in various situations.
- Middle East and Asia: don't point with one finger (it's rude); use your whole hand.
- New Zealand: tipping is not customary, and your tip may be refused.
- Peru: raised eyebrows mean "pay me."
- Saudi Arabia: be sure to tip your taxi driver.
- Singapore and Malaysia: offer gifts with the right hand only.
- Taiwan: blinking is considered impolite.

adapted from Roger E. Axtell, ed.,
Do's and Taboos Around the World

❧ SHOPPING AND SHIPPING ❧

By the time I've visited four or five shops, I
know a lot about Italian politics, football,
which grapes make good Chianti, and how to
make good pumpkin soup.

KERRY FISHER, IN ITALY

(See Customs information on page 21.)

- Guides are often essential in souks and bazaars, but be aware of how they operate: they will keep you from getting lost and show you to shops that sell what you want to buy, but they are often on commission from shopkeepers and so have an interest in showing you to certain shops. Trust your instincts in selecting a guide, and fix your price in advance. If you decide to chance it alone, be aware that the fellow who tags along after you and stands in the doorway of the shop may later hit the shopkeeper up for a commission—make it clear to the shopkeeper that he is not your guide and is not entitled to a commission, and you may be able to strike a better deal.

- Start your bartering at a quarter of the price the shopkeeper names—half his or her price will likely still be a bargain.

- Buy tax-free and duty-free items such as perfume and liquor in airports and on ferries, planes, and trains that cross international borders. International airports have the best selection.

- Hamilton, Bermuda and Ushaia, Argentina are duty-free ports: liquor stores will package up your purchases and send them directly to the airport, where they will be put on your flight.

- In Britain, remember to keep receipts for clothing and other substantial purchases: you can reclaim the hefty Value Added Tax (VAT) after you leave the country.

- Shops will often arrange for shipping your non-portable purchases to your home; however it may be cheaper to arrange your own shipping. Ask at your hotel for a reputable shipper or freight forwarder.

adapted in part from Globe Pequot Press's
The Traveler's Handbook

❧ DRESS ❧

Compared with the other women, I was a complete oaf and indeed, hardly female. I was clumsy at cutting bamboo or vegetables...unable to light the fire, and hopelessly inelegant in a sari.

KATY GARDNER, IN BANGLADESH

Be aware of dress standards in the countries you visit. In much of the world, women's dress codes are more restrictive, or, at least, different than those Western women are used to. It is worthwhile remembering that miniskirts in Istanbul, shorts in Marrakech, and torn t-shirts in Singapore will be taken as signs of disrespect, if nothing worse, and may create more headaches than you bargained for. Realize you may not be allowed to enter places of worship if you are improperly dressed, and that in strict Muslim countries such as Iran, you may even be arrested or forced to cover up.

adapted from Globe Pequot Press's *The Traveler's Handbook*

❧ CONVERSION CHARTS ☙

WEIGHT
1 ounce = 28.3 grams
1 gram = .035 ounce
1 pound = .454 kilogram
1 kilogram = 2.2 pounds

VOLUME
1 pint = .571 liter
1 liter = 1.76 pints

LENGTH/DISTANCE
1 inch = 2.54 centimeters
1 centimeter = .394 inch
1 foot = .3 meter
1 meter = 3.28 feet
1 mile = 1.61 kilometers
1 kilometer = .62 mile

TEMPERATURE

°F	- 40	32	41	50	59	68	86	100	104
°C	- 40	0	5	10	15	20	30	38	40

Simple formulas for converting temperature:
$(C \times 2) + 30 = F$; $(F - 32) / 2 = C$

VOLTAGES AND PLUGS

There is a wide variation in voltages and plug configuration worldwide; here are some regional standards.

North America
110 volts

Asia
220 volts

South and Central America
110 or 220 volts

Southeast Asia
110-220 volts

Continental Europe
220 volts (two-pin plug)

Africa
220-380 volts

United Kingdom
240 volts (three-pin plug)

Australia
240 volts

India and Nepal
220 volts (some areas need invertors)

❧ Clothing Sizes ❧

Women's Clothing

Dresses, Suits, Coats, Sweaters, etc

Canada/US	4	6	8	10	12	14	16	18
UK/Australia	6	8	10	12	14	16	18	20
Japan	7	9	11	13				
Continental Europe	32	34	36	38	40	42	44	46

Shoes

Canada/US/ Australia	5	5½	6	6½	7	7½	8	8½	9	9½	10
UK	3½	4	4½	5	5½	6	6½	7	7½	8	8½
Continental Europe	36	36	37	37	38	38	39	39	40	40	40

Men's Clothing

Suits, Jackets, Sweaters, etc

Canada/US/UK	34	36	38	40	42	44	46
Continental Europe/ Australia	44	46	48	50	52	54	56
Japan	S	M	L	XL			

Shirts

Canada/US/UK	14½	15	15½	16	16½	17	17½	18
Continental Europe/ Australia/Japan	37	38	39	41	42	43	44	45

Shoes

Canada/US	7½	8	8½	9	9½	10	10½	11
UK/Australia	7	7½	8	8½	9	9½	10	10 ½
Continental Europe	40	41	42	43	43	44	44	45

❧ INTERNATIONAL DIALING COUNTRY CODES ❧

To place a call to a foreign country dial: 1. *international
direct dial code* 2. *country code* 3. *area code* 4. *number*
For example, to call Malaysia from New York,
dial 011 60 3 261 2000

Country	Country Code	Country	Country Code	Country	Country Code
Algeria	213	Honduras	504	Paraguay	595
Andorra	33	Hong Kong	852	Peru	51
Argentina	54	Hungary	36	Philippines	63
Australia	61	Iceland	354	Poland	48
Austria	43	India	91	Portugal	351
Bahamas	809	Indonesia	62	Romania	40
Belgium	32	Iran	98	Russia	7
Bosnia and		Iraq	964	Saudi Arabia	966
Herzegovina	387	Ireland	058	Senegal	221
Brazil	55	Israel	972	Serbia	381
Burma	95	Italy	39	Singapore	65
Cameroon	237	Japan	81	Slovakia	42
Canada	1	Jordan	962	Slovenia	386
Chile	56	Kenya	254	South Africa	27
China	86	Korea (North		Spain	34
Colombia	57	and South)	82	Sri Lanka	94
Costa Rica	506	Kuwait	965	Sweden	46
Côte d'Ivoire	225	Latvia	371	Switzerland	41
Croatia	385	Lebanon	961	Syria	963
Cyprus	357	Liberia	231	Taiwan	886
Czech Republic	42	Libya	218	Tanzania	255
Denmark	45	Liechtenstein	41	Thailand	66
Ecuador	593	Luxembourg	352	Tunisia	216
Egypt	20	Malaysia	60	Turkey	90
El Salvador	503	Mexico	52	Uganda	256
Eritrea	291	Monaco	33	Ukraine	7
Ethiopia	251	Morocco	212	United Arab Emirates	971
Fiji	679	Nepal	977	United Kingdom	44
Finland	358	Netherlands	31	United States	1
France	33	New Zealand	64	Uruguay	598
Germany	49	Nicaragua	505	Venezuela	58
Greece	30	Nigeria	231	Vietnam	84
Guam	671	Norway	47	Zaire	243
Guatemala	502	Pakistan	92	Zambia	260
Guyana	592	Papua New Guinea	675	Zimbabwe	263
Haiti	509				

✤ WORLD CURRENCIES AND LANGUAGES ✤

Country
Currency
Languages

Afghanistan
Afghani: 100 Puls
Pashtu, Dari Uzbek,
  Turkmen

Albania
Lek: 100 Qintars
Albanian, Greek

Algeria
Dinar: 100 Centimes
Arabic, Berber dialects,
  French

Angola
Kwanza: 100 Lwei
Portuguese, indigenous

Australia
Dollar: 100 Cents
English

Austria
Schilling: 100 Groschen
German

Bahrain
Dinar: 1000 Fils
Arabic, English, Farsi, Urdu

Bangladesh
Taka: 100 Poish
Bangla, English

Belgium
Franc: 100 Centimes
French, Dutch, German

Bhutan
Ngultrum: 100 Chetrum
Dzongkha, Nepalese
  and Tibetan dialects

Botswana
Pula: 100 Thebe
English, Tswana

Brazil
Cruzeiro: 100 Centavos
Portuguese

Bulgaria
Lev: 100 Stotinki
Bulgarian

Burma
Kyat: 100 Pyas
Burmese, English

Cambodia
Riel: 100 Sen
Khmer, French

Cameroon
Franc: 100 Centimes
French, English, Bantu

Canada
Dollar; 100 Cents
English, French

Chad
Franc: 100 Centimes
Arabic, French

Chile
Peso: 100 Centavos
Spanish

China
Yuan: 100 Fen
Chinese dialects

Colombia
Peso: 100 Centavos
Spanish

Congo
Franc: 100 Centimes
French, Lingala,
  Kikongo

Côte d'Ivoire
Franc: 100 Centimes
French, indigenous

Cuba
Peso: 100 Centavos
Spanish

Cyprus
Pound: 100 Cents
Greek, Turkish, English

Czech Republic
Koruny: 100 Haleru
Czech

Denmark
Kroner: 100 Ore
Danish

Ecuador
Sucre: 100 Centavos
Spanish, Quechua,
  indigenous

Egypt
Pound: 100 Piastres
Arabic, English, French

El Salvador
Colon: 100 Centavos
Spanish, Nahua

Ethiopia
Birr: 100 Cents
Amharic, Tigre, Afar,
  Galla

Fiji
Dollar: 100 Cents
English, Fijian,
  Hindustani

Finland
Markka: 100 Pennia
Finnish, Swedish

France
Franc: 100 Centimes
French

Gambia
Dalasi: 100 Bututs
English, Malinke,
  Wolof, Fula

Germany
Deutschemark: 100
  Pfennige
German

Ghana
Cedi: 100 Pesewas
English, Twi, Fanti, Ga Ewe

Greece
Drachma: 100 Leptae
Greek

Guatemala
Quetzal:100 Centavos
Spanish, indigenous

Guyana
Dollar: 100 Cents
English, Hindi, patois

Honduras
Lempira: 100 Centavos
Spanish, indigenous

Hungary
Forint: 100 Filler
Hungarian

Iceland
Krona: 100 Aurar
Icelandic

India
Rupee: 100 Paise
Hindi, English, Telugu,
  Bengali, over 70
  dialects

Indonesia
Rupiah: 100 Sen
Bahasa Indonesia, 250
  regional languages

Iran
Rial: 100 Dinars
Farsi, Kurdish, Luri,
  Baluchi, Turkic
  languages

Iraq
Dinar: 1000 Fils
Arabic, Kurdish,
  Assyrian, Armenian

Ireland
Irish Punt: 100 Pence
Irish, English

Israel
Shekel: 100 Agorot
Hebrew, Arabic, Yiddish

Italy
Lira: 100 Centesimi
Italian

Jamaica
Dollar: 100 Cents
English, Creole

Japan
Yen: 100 Sen
Japanese

Jordan
Dinar: 1000 Fils
Arabic

Kenya
Shilling: 100 Cents
Swahili, English,
  indigenous

Korea
  (North and South)
Won: 100 Chon
Korean

Kuwait
Dinar: 1000 Fils
Arabic, English

Laos
Kip: 100 Att
Lao, French, indigenous

Lebanon
Pound: 100 Piastres
Arabic, French,
  Armenian, English

Lesotho
Loti: 100 Lisente
Sesotho, English, Zulu,
  Xhosa

Liberia
Dollar: 100 Cents
English, indigenous

Libya
Dinar: 1000 Dirhams
Arabic, Berber dialects

Liechtenstein
Franc: 100 Rappen
German

Luxembourg
Franc: 100 Centimes
French, Luxembourgish,
  German

Madagascar
Franc: 100 Centimes
Malagasy, French,
  English

Malaysia
Ringgit: 100 Sen
Malay, English, Chinese,
  Tamil, indigenous

Mexico
Peso: 100 Centavos
Spanish, indigenous

Monaco
Franc: 100 Centimes
French, Monegasque,
  English, Italian

Morocco
Dirham: 100 Centimes
Arabic, Spanish, Berber
  dialects, French

Mozambique
Metical: 100 Centavos
Portuguese, indigenous

Nepal
Rupee: 100 Paisa
Nepali, Newari, Maithili,
  Bhojpuri, Tibetan
  dialects

Netherlands
Guilder: 100 Cents
Dutch

New Zealand
Dollar: 100 Cents
English, Maori

Nicaragua
Cordoba: 100 Centavos
Spanish, English,
  Chibcha, indigenous

Niger
Franc: 100 Centimes
French, Hausa, Djerma,
  indigenous

Nigeria
Naira: 100 Kobo
English, Hausa, Ibo,
  Yoruba, Fulani,
  indigenous

Norway
Krone: 100 Ore
Norwegian, Lapp

❧ WORLD CURRENCIES AND LANGUAGES ❧

Pakistan
Rupee: 100 Paise
Urdu, Punjabi, English,
  Pashto, Sindhi, Saraiki

Papua New Guinea
Kina: 100 Toea
English, Motu, Pidgin,
  indigenous

Paraguay
Guarani: 100 Centimos
Spanish, Guarani

Philippines
Peso: 100 Centavos
Philipino, English,
  Spanish, Tagalog

Poland
Zloty: 100 Groszy
Polish

Portugal
Escudo: 100 Centavos
Portuguese

Romania
Leu: 100 Bani
Romanian, Hungarian,
  German

Russia
Ruble: 100 Kopeks
Russian, Tatar, Ukrainian

Saudi Arabia
Riyal: 100 Halalas
Arabic

Senegal
Franc: 100 Centimes
French, Wolof, Fulani,
  indigenous

Singapore
Dollar: 100 Sen
Malay, Chinese, Tamil,
  English

Slovakia
Koruny: 100 Haleru
Slovak

Solomon Islands
Dollar: 100 Cents
English, Malay
  Polynesian languages

Somalia
Shilling: 100 Cents
Somali, Arabic, Italian,
  English

South Africa
Rand: 100 Cents
Afrikaans, English,
  Xhosa, Zulu, Swazi,
  indigenous

Spain
Peseta: 100 Centimos
Spanish, Catalan,
  Galician, Basque

Sri Lanka
Rupee: 100 Cents
Sinhala, English, Tamil

Sudan
Pound: 100 Piastres,
  1000 Milliemes
Arabic, English, indigenous

Sweden
Krona: 100 Ore
Swedish

Switzerland
Franc: 100 Centimes
German, French, Italian,
  Romansch

Syria
Pound: 100 Piastres
Arabic, Kurdish,
  Armenian, Aramaic,
  Circassian

Taiwan
Dollar: 100 Cents
Chinese dialects

Tanzania
Shilling: 100 Senti
Swahili, English, indigenous

Thailand
Baht: 100 Satangs
Thai, English, indigenous

Tonga
Pa'anga: 100 Seniti
Tongan, English

Tunisia
Dinar: 100 Millimes
Arabic, French

Turkey
Lira: 100 Kurus
Turkish, Kurdish, Arabic

Uganda
Shilling: 100 Cents
English, Swahili,
  Luganda, indigenous

United Arab Emirates
Dirham: 1000 Fils
Arabic, English, Hindi,
  Farsi, Urdu

United Kingdom
Pound: 100 Pence
English, Welsh, Gaelic

Uruguay
Peso: 100 Centesimos
Spanish

United States of America
Dollar: 100 Cents
English

Venezuela
Bolivar: 100 Centimos
Spanish, indigenous

Vietnam
Dong: 10 Hao, 100 Xu
Vietnamese, French, English,
  Chinese, Khmer, indigenous

Western Samoa
Tala: 100 Sene
Samoan, English

Zaire
Zaire: 100 Makuta
French, Swahili, Kikongo,
  Lingala, Tshiluba

Zambia
Kwacha: 100 Ngwee
English, Tonga, Lozi,
  indigenous

Zimbabwe
Dollar: 100 Cents
English, ChiShona, SiNdebele

❦ WORLD CLIMATES ❦

Temperatures are in degrees Fahrenheit. (Avg. high/avg. low)

LOCATION	Jan-Mar	Apr-Jun	Jul-Sep	Oct-Dec
Acapulco	88/72	90/77	90/75	90/72
Athens	60/44	86/52	92/67	75/47
Bangkok	93/68	95/76	90/76	88/68
Berlin	46/26	72/39	75/50	56/29
Bermuda	68/57	81/59	85/72	79/60
Bogotá	68/48	67/51	66/49	66/49
Boston	43/20	75/38	80/55	62/25
Buenos Aires	85/60	72/41	64/42	82/50
Cairo	75/47	95/57	96/68	86/50
Calcutta	93/55	97/75	90/78	89/55
Caracas	79/56	81/60	80/61	79/58
Chicago	43/18	75/40	81/58	88/23
Dallas	67/36	90/55	94/68	78/38
Dublin	51/34	65/39	67/48	57/37
Hong Kong	67/55	85/67	87/77	81/59
Honolulu	77/67	81/68	83/73	82/69
Jerusalem	65/41	85/50	87/62	81/45
Istanbul	51/37	77/45	82/61	68/41
Kathmandu	77/35	86/53	84/66	80/37
Las Vegas	72/29	99/45	103/57	84/30
Lima	83/66	80/58	68/56	78/58
Lisbon	63/46	77/53	82/62	72/47
London	50/36	69/42	71/52	58/38
Los Angeles	67/46	76/50	82/58	76/47

LOCATION	Jan-Mar	Apr-Jun	Jul-Sep	Oct-Dec
Madrid	59/35	80/45	87/57	65/36
Manila	91/69	93/73	88/75	88/70
Mexico City	75/42	78/51	74/53	70/43
Montevideo	83/59	71/43	63/43	79/49
Munich	48/23	70/38	74/48	56/26
Nairobi	79/54	75/53	75/51	76/55
Miami	78/61	86/67	88/75	83/62
Nassau	79/64	87/69	90/75	85/67
New Orleans	71/47	88/61	90/73	79/48
New York City	45/24	77/42	82/60	69/29
Paris	54/34	73/43	76/53	60/36
Phoenix	75/39	101/53	104/69	86/40
Port-au-Prince	89/68	92/71	94/73	90/69
Quito	72/46	71/45	73/44	72/45
Rio de Janeiro	85/72	80/64	76/63	82/66
Rome	59/40	82/50	87/62	71/44
St. Lucia	84/69	88/71	88/73	87/70
San Francisco	61/45	66/49	69/53	68/47
Santa Fe	51/19	78/35	80/49	62/20
Santiago	85/49	74/37	66/37	83/45
Seattle	52/36	69/43	72/52	59/38
Seoul	47/15	80/41	87/59	67/20
Singapore	88/73	89/75	88/75	87/74
Taipei	70/53	89/63	92/73	81/57
Tokyo	54/29	76/46	86/66	69/33
Toronto	37/15	73/34	79/51	56/21
Vancouver	50/32	69/40	74/49	57/35
Washington, DC	53/27	83/44	87/59	67/29

❧ FLIGHT TIMES AND DISTANCES BETWEEN CITIES ❧
(approximate)

From - To	Hours	Miles	From - To	Hours	Miles
Chicago - Amsterdam	7:50	4109	New York - New Delhi	16:00	7349
Chicago - Auckland	18:30	8268	New York - Paris	7:10	3630
Chicago - Bangkok	21:30	8548	New York - Rio de Janeiro	11:30	4816
Chicago - Buenos Aires	13:00	5607	New York - Rome	8:00	4280
Chicago - Frankfurt	8:50	4332	New York - San Jose	7:00	2215
Chicago - Hong Kong	19:30	7827	New York - Singapore	21:30	9886
Chicago - London	8:10	3950	New York - Sydney	21:00	9957
Chicago - Mexico City	4:00	1687	New York - Tokyo	14:00	6737
Chicago - New Delhi	17:30	7488	Toronto - Amsterdam	7:00	3720
Chicago - Paris	8:05	4142	Toronto - Auckland	20:00	8696
Chicago - Rio de Janeiro	10:45	5302	Toronto - Bangkok	25:00	9110
Chicago - Rome	9:10	4816	Toronto - Buenos Aires	12:30	5584
Chicago - San Jose	7:00	2287	Toronto - Frankfurt	7:35	3939
Chicago - Singapore	21:00	9426	Toronto - Hong Kong	19:00	8108
Chicago - Sydney	20:00	9244	Toronto - London	7:00	3553
Chicago - Tokyo	13:00	6286	Toronto - Mexico City	7:00	2020
L.A. - Amsterdam	10:30	5559	Toronto - New Delhi	17:00	7488
L.A. - Auckland	12:45	6522	Toronto - Paris	7:00	3739
L.A. - Bangkok	19:00	8249	Toronto - Rio de Janeiro	12:30	5756
L.A. - Buenos Aires	16:00	6140	Toronto - Rome	9:30	4407
L.A. - Frankfurt	11:00	5786	Toronto - San Jose	9:00	2336
L.A. - Hong Kong	14:30	7277	Toronto - Singapore	24:00	9288
L.A. - London	10:30	5442	Toronto - Sydney	26:30	9672
L.A. - Mexico City	3:30	1563	Toronto - Tokyo	17:00	6419
L.A. - New Delhi	21:00	8011	Vancouver - Amsterdam	7:00	4791
L.A. - Paris	10:45	5654	Vancouver - Auckland	20:00	7112
L.A. - Rio de Janeiro	15:00	6311	Vancouver - Bangkok	16:30	7374
L.A. - Rome	12:00	6340	Vancouver - Buenos Aires	21:00	7005
L.A. - San Jose	7:00	2734	Vancouver - Frankfurt	11:30	5011
L.A. - Singapore	19:00	8764	Vancouver - Hong Kong	13:00	6371
L.A. - Sydney	14:30	7498	Vancouver - London	9:00	4713
L.A. - Tokyo	11:30	5451	Vancouver - Mexico City	7:00	2452
New York - Amsterdam	7:20	3639	Vancouver - New Delhi	19:00	8882
New York - Auckland	20:00	8809	Vancouver - Paris	12:30	4932
New York - Bangkok	19:00	9172	Vancouver - Rio de Janeiro	18:00	6963
New York - Buenos Aires	11:00	5302	Vancouver - Rome	15:00	5612
New York - Frankfurt	7:30	3851	Vancouver - San Jose	11:30	3508
New York - Hong Kong	20:00	8170	Vancouver - Singapore	18:00	7966
New York - London	6:45	3458	Vancouver - Sydney	19:00	7769
New York - Mexico City	5:00	2086	Vancouver - Tokyo	9:40	4681

❧ DISTANCES FROM AIRPORTS TO CITIES ❧

*Should we have stayed at home and
thought of here?*

ELIZABETH BISHOP

Country	City	Airport	Distance (miles)
Argentina	Buenos Aires	Ministro Pistarini International	20
Australia	Melbourne	Melbourne	11
	Perth	International	6
	Sydney	Kingsford Smith	5
Austria	Vienna	Schwechat	11
Belgium	Brussels	National	10
Brazil	Rio De Janeiro	Galeao International	6
Canada	Montreal	Mirabel	33
	Toronto	Malton	17
China	Beijing	Capital	18
Costa Rica	San Jose	Juan Santamaria International	10
Fiji	Suva	Nausori	14
France	Paris	Charles de Gaulle	18
		Orly	9
Germany	Berlin	Tegel	5
	Frankfurt	Rhein-Main	7
	Hamburg	Fuhlsbuttel	7
Greece	Athens	Hellinikon	7
India	New Delhi	Indira Gandhi International	13
Indonesia	Jakarta	Halim Perdanakusuma International	5
	Bali	Nguran Rai	8
Ireland	Dublin	Dublin	5
Italy	Rome	Leonardo da Vinci	19

🌿 DISTANCES FROM AIRPORTS TO CITIES 🌿
(continued)

Country	City	Airport	Distance (miles)
Japan	Tokyo	Narita	40
	Osaka	Itami International	12
Malaysia	Kuala Lumpur	Subang	13
	Penang	Bayan Lepas	11
Mexico	Mexico City	Benito Juarez	8
Netherlands	Amsterdam	Schipol International	8
New Zealand	Wellington	Rongotoi	5
	Auckland	International	13
Philippines	Manila	International	7
Russia	Moscow	Sheremetievo	16
Singapore	Singapore	Changi	12
South Africa	Johannesburg	Jan Smuts	18
Spain	Madrid	Barajas	7
Sweden	Stockholm	Arlanda	25
Switzerland	Geneva	Cointrin	2
	Zurich	Kloten	7
Thailand	Bangkok	Don Muang	13
United Kingdom	London	Gatwick	26
		Heathrow	14
United States	Honolulu	International	8
	Los Angeles	International	14
	New York	J F Kennedy International	14
		La Guardia	8
		Newark International	16
	San Francisco	International	16

❧ AMERICAN AND CANADIAN EMBASSIES ❧

A complete list of embassies, high commissions and consulates can
be had from your government printing office: (202) 512 1800 for
US; (800) 567-6868 for Canadian.

Phone numbers given with city codes, if any, in ( );
for country codes, see page 136.

Country	US Embassy	Canadian Embassy
Argentina	4300 Colombia, 1425 Buenos Aires (1) 777-4533	Tagle 2828 Buenos Aires (1) 805-3032
Australia	Moonah Pl Canberra (6) 270-5000	Canadian High Commission Commonwealth Ave Canberra (6) 273-3844
Austria	Boltzmanngasse 16 Vienna (1) 313-39	Schubertring 10 Vienna (222) 533-3691
Belgium	27 Boulevard du Regent Brussels (2) 508-2111	2 av de Tervuren Brussels (2) 735-6040
Brazil	Avenida das Naçcoes, Lote 3 Brasilia (61) 321-7272	Setor de Embaixadas Sul Avenida das Naçcoes, Lote 16 Brasilia (61) 321-2171
Canada	100 Wellington St Ottawa (613) 238-4470	
Costa Rica	Pavas San Jose (506) 220-3939	Edificio Cronos Calle 3y Av Central San Jose (506) 55-35-22
Czech Republic	Trziste 15 Prague (2) 536-641	Mickiewiczova 6 Prague (2) 2431-1108
Denmark	Dag Hammarskjolds Alle 24 Copenhagen 31-42-31-44	Kr Bernikowsgade Copenhagen 33-12-22-99
Egypt	8 Kamal El-Din Salah St Garden City Cairo (2) 355-7371	6 Mohamed Fahmy el Sayed St Garden City Cairo (2) 354-3110

❧ AMERICAN AND CANADIAN EMBASSIES ❧
(continued)

Country	US Embassy	Canadian Embassy
Finland	Itainen Puistotie 14A Helsinki (0) 17-19-31	P Esplanadi 25B Helsinki (0) 17-11-41
France	2 Avenue Gabriel Paris (1) 43-12-22-22	35 Avenue Montaigne Paris (1) 44-43-29-00
Germany	Deichmanns Aue 29 Bonn (228) 3391	Friedrich-Wilhelm-Strasse 18 Bonn (228) 9680
Greece	91 Vasilissis Sophias Blvd Athens (1) 721-2951	4 Ioannu Ghennadiou St Athens (1) 725-4011
Hong Kong	Consulate General 26 Garden Rd 2523-9011	Commission for Canada 11-14th Fls, 1 Exchange Sq 8 Connaught Pl 810-4321
Hungary	V Szabadsag Ter 12 Budapest (1) 267-4400	Budakeszi ut 32 Budapest (1) 1767-312
India	Shantipath Chanakyapuri New Delhi (11) 600-651	Canadian High Commission 7/8 Shantipath Chanakyapuri New Delhi (11) 687-6500
Indonesia	Medan Merdeka Selatan 5 Jakarta (21) 36-03-60	5th Fl, WISMA Metropolitan 1 Jalan Jendral Sudirman Kav 29 Jakarta (21) 51-07-09
Ireland	42 Elgin Road Ballsbridge Dublin (1) 6687122	65 St Stephens Green Dublin (1) 78-19-88
Israel	71 Rehov Hayarkon Tel Aviv (3) 517-4338	220 Rehov Hayarkon Tel Aviv (3) 527-2929
Italy	Via Veneto 119/A Rome (6) 46741	Via G.B. de Rossi 27 Rome (6) 841-5341
Japan	10-5 Akasaka 1-chome Minato-ku Tokyo (3) 3224-5000	3-38 Akasaka 7-chome Minato-ku Tokyo (3) 3408-2101
Korea (South)	82 Sejong-Ro Chongro-ku Seoul (2) 397-4114	45 Mugyo-Dong Jung-Ku Seoul (2) 753-2605

❧ AMERICAN AND CANADIAN EMBASSIES ❧
(continued)

Country	US Embassy	Canadian Embassy
Malaysia	376 Jalan Tun Razak Kuala Lumpur (3) 248-9011	Canadian High Commission 172 Jalan Ampang Kuala Lumpur (3) 261-2000
Mexico	Paseo de la Reforma 305 Mexico City (5) 211-0042	Calle Schiller 529 Col Rincon del Bosque Mexico City (5) 724-7900
Morocco	2 Ave de Marrakech Rabat (7) 76-22-65	13 Bis, Rue Jaafar As Sadik Rabat (7) 77-28-80
Nepal	Pani Pokhari Kathmandu (1) 411179	c/o India
Netherlands	Lange Voorhout 102 The Hague (70) 310-9209	Sophialaan 7 The Hague (70) 351-4111
New Zealand	29 Fitzherbert Terrace Thorndon Wellington (4) 472-2068	Canadian High Commission 61 Molesworth St Thorndon Wellington (4) 473-9577
Norway	Drammensveien 18 Oslo 22-44-85-50	Oscar's Gate 20 Oslo 22-46-69-55
Poland	Aleje Ujazdowskie 29/31 Warsaw (22) 628-3041	Ulica Matejki 1/5 Strodmiescle Warsaw (22) 29-80-51
Portugal	Avenida das Forcas Armadas Lisbon (1) 726-6600	Avenida da Liberdade 144/56 Lisbon (1) 347-4892
Russia	Novinskiy Bul'var 19/23 Moscow (095) 252-2451	23 Starokonyushenny Pereulok Moscow (095) 241-1111
Singapore	30 Hill St 338-0251	Canadian High Commission 80 Anson Rd 225-6363
Slovakia	Hviezdoslavovo Namestie 4 Bratislava (7) 330861	c/o Czech Republic
South Africa	877 Pretorius St Pretoria (12) 342-1048	Nedbank Plaza 5th Fl Church & Beatrix Sts Arcadia, Pretoria (12) 324-3970

❧ AMERICAN AND CANADIAN EMBASSIES ❧
(continued)

Country	US Embassy	Canadian Embassy
Spain	Serrano 75 Madrid (1) 577-4000	Edificio Goya Calle Nunez de Balboa 35 Madrid (1) 431-4300
Sweden	Strandvagen 101 Stockholm (8) 783-5300	Tegelbacken 4 Stockholm (8) 613-9900
Switzerland	Jubilaeumstrasse 93 Bern (31) 357-7011	Kirchenfeldstrasse 88 Bern (31) 352-63-81
Thailand	95 Wireless Rd Bangkok (2) 252-5040	138 Silom Rd Bangkok (2) 237-4125
Turkey	110 Ataturk Blvd Ankara (4) 468-6110	75 Nenehatun Caddesi Gaziosmanpasa Ankara (4) 436-1275
Ukraine	10 Yuria Kotsyubinskovo Kiev (044) 244-7349	31 Yaroslaviv Val St Kiev (044) 212-2112
United Kingdom	24/31 Grosvenor Sq London (171) 499-9000	Canadian High Commission 1 Grosvenor Sq London (171) 658-6600
United States		501 Pennsylvania Ave NW Washington, DC (202) 682-1740

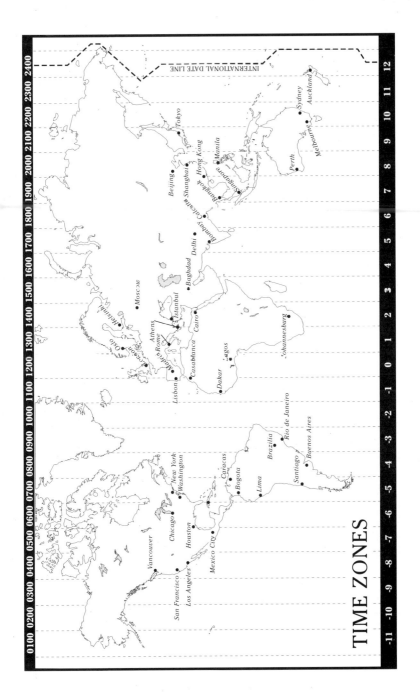

TIME ZONES

INTERNATIONAL DATE LINE

0100 0200 0300 0400 0500 0600 0700 0800 0900 1000 1100 1200 1300 1400 1500 1600 1700 1800 1900 2000 2100 2200 2300 2400

-11 -10 -9 -8 -7 -6 -5 -4 -3 -2 -1 0 1 2 3 4 5 6 7 8 9 10 11 12

Vancouver · San Francisco · Los Angeles · Houston · Mexico City · Chicago · New York · Washington · Caracas · Bogota · Lima · Brazilia · Rio de Janeiro · Santiago · Buenos Aires · Dakar · Casablanca · Lisbon · Oslo · Stockholm · Helsinki · Madrid · Rome · Athens · Istanbul · Moscow · Lagos · Johannesburg · Cairo · Baghdad · Delhi · Bombay · Calcutta · Bangkok · Hong Kong · Shanghai · Beijing · Singapore · Manila · Tokyo · Perth · Melbourne · Sydney · Auckland

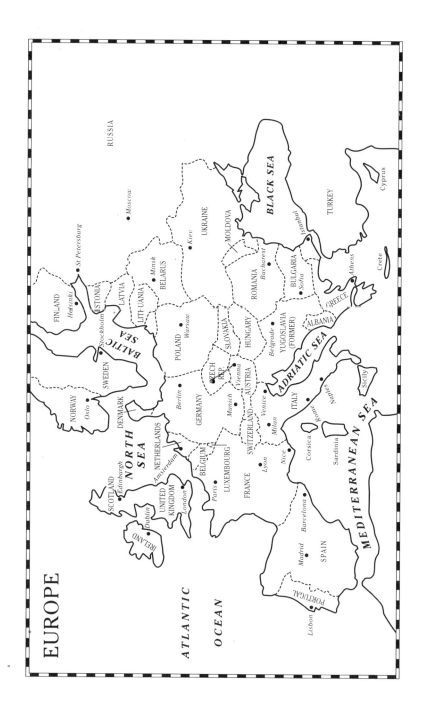

EUROPE

ATLANTIC

OCEAN

RUSSIA

NORTH SEA

BALTIC SEA

BLACK SEA

MEDITERRANEAN SEA

ADRIATIC SEA

FINLAND
Helsinki

St Petersburg

Moscow

ESTONIA

LATVIA

LITH-UANIA

Minsk

BELARUS

SWEDEN
Stockholm

NORWAY
Oslo

DENMARK

Kiev

UKRAINE

MOLDOVA

POLAND
Warsaw

Berlin

GERMANY

SLOVAKIA

CZECH REP.

Vienna

AUSTRIA

HUNGARY

ROMANIA
Bucharest

BULGARIA
Sofia

YUGOSLAVIA
(FORMER)

Belgrade

ALBANIA

GREECE

TURKEY

Istanbul

Athens

Crete

Cyprus

NETHERLANDS
Amsterdam

Munich

SWITZERLAND

Venice

Milan

Venice

ITALY

Rome

Naples

Sardinia

Corsica

Sicily

SCOTLAND
Edinburgh

UNITED KINGDOM
London

IRELAND
Dublin

BELGIUM

LUXEMBOURG

Paris

FRANCE

Lyon

Nice

SPAIN
Madrid

Barcelona

PORTUGAL

Lisbon

· 150 ·

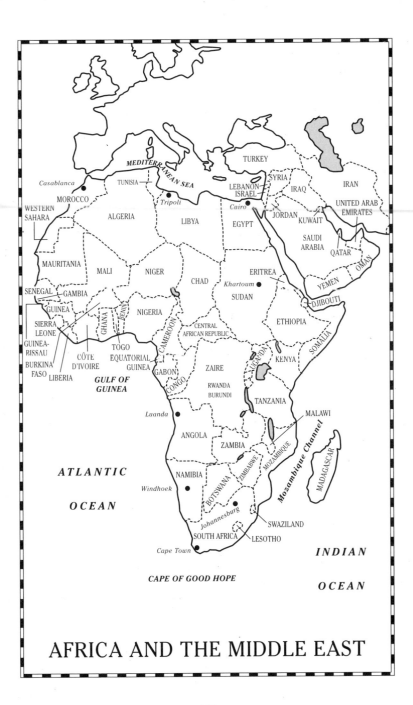

AFRICA AND THE MIDDLE EAST

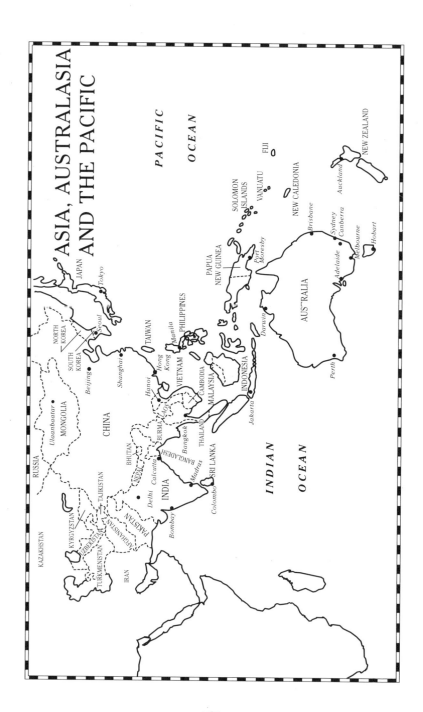

ASIA, AUSTRALASIA
AND THE PACIFIC

PACIFIC

OCEAN

RUSSIA

KAZAKHSTAN

MONGOLIA
Ulaanbaatar

JAPAN
Tokyo

NORTH
KOREA
SOUTH
KOREA
Seoul

Beijing

Shanghai

KYRGYZSTAN
UZBEKISTAN
TURKMENISTAN
TAJIKISTAN
AFGHANISTAN

CHINA

TAIWAN

Hanoi

Hong
Kong

Manila

PHILIPPINES

IRAN

PAKISTAN

BHUTAN
NEPAL

Delhi

BANGLADESH
Calcutta

BURMA

LAOS

VIETNAM

CAMBODIA

Bangkok

THAILAND

MALAYSIA

INDONESIA

Bombay

INDIA

Madras

SRI LANKA
Colombo

Jakarta

INDIAN

OCEAN

Darwin

PAPUA
NEW GUINEA

Port
Moresby

SOLOMON
ISLANDS

VANUATU

FIJI

NEW CALEDONIA

AUSTRALIA

Brisbane

Sydney
Canberra

Adelaide

Melbourne

Hobart

Perth

NEW ZEALAND

Auckland

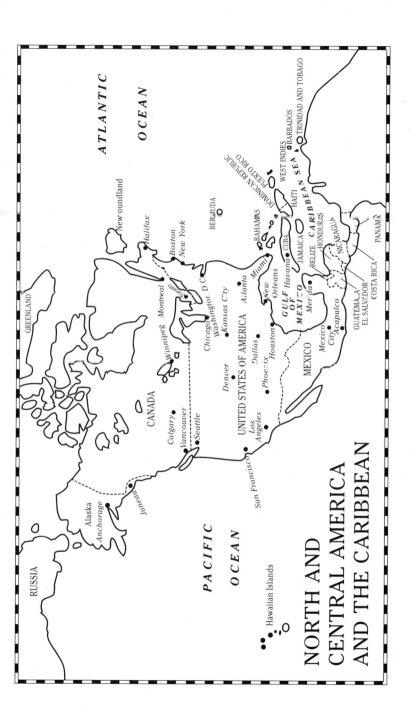

NORTH AND
CENTRAL AMERICA
AND THE CARIBBEAN

SOUTH AMERICA

❧ RESOURCES ❧

Books

GUIDES AND REFERENCE

- *Adventures in Good Company: The Complete Guide to Women's Tours and Outdoor Trips*, by Thalia Zepatos. Eighth Mountain Press, 1994.

  An excellent introduction to hundreds of organizations that cater to women adventure travelers, students, older women, disabled women, women traveling with children, lesbians, and more. Packed with the advice and personal perspectives of dozens of women.

- *Do's and Taboos Around the World*, ed. by Roger E. Axtell. John Wiley & Sons, 1993.

  A guide to etiquette in various countries for the American who travels abroad for business.

- The Feminist Press has a women's travel series covering individual countries, including Greece, China, and Australia.

- *The Independent Woman's Guide to Europe*, by Linda White. Fulcrum Publishing, 1991.

  Tips for women from a veteran traveler.

- *Jet Smart*, by Diana Fairechilde. Celestial Arts, 1994.

  The ultimate guide to avoiding jet lag.

- *A Journey of One's Own: Uncommon Advice for the Independent Woman Traveler*, by Thalia Zepatos. Eighth Mountain Press, 1992.

  An excellent resource for women travelers, with sound advice on safety, traveling alone or with children, traveling while pregnant, tips for older women, and more. Good bibliography.

- *The Packing Book*, by Judith Gilford. Ten Speed Press, 1994.

  How to pack for any kind of trip. Will cure the chronic over-packer.

- *The Rough Guide Specials to Women Travel: More Women Travel*, Viking Penguin, 1995.

  A wonderful mix of the personal experiences of dozens of independent women travel writers with resources for women travelers in over 60 countries. Third in a series.

- *The Traveler's Handbook: The Essential Guide for International Travelers, 6th Ed.*, ed. by Caroline Brandenburger. Globe Pequot Press, 1994.

  A truly exhaustive, but lively compendium of information, advice, and resources for every kind of traveler to just about any place in the world. Small section specifically for women.

- *Virago Woman's Travel Guides*, distributed by RDR Books.

  Excellent guides for women traveling in selected cities.

- *Women's Guide to Overseas Living*, by Nancy Piet-Pelon and Barbara Hornby. Intercultural Press, 1993.

  The practicalities of living overseas.

TRAVEL WRITING

- *The House on Via Gombito: Writing by North American Women Abroad*, ed. by Madelon Sprengnether and C.W. Truesdale. New Rivers Press, 1991.

  A highly readable anthology of writings by Canadian and American writers.

- *Maiden Voyages*, ed. by Mary Morris. Vintage, 1992.

  Extracts from the works of some of the greatest Western women travel writers, from Lady Mary Wortley Montagu to Beryl Markham.

- *The Traveler's Reading Guide: Ready-Made Reading Lists for the Armchair Traveler*, ed. by Maggy Simony. Facts on File, 1993.

- *Traveler's Tales: A Woman's World*, ed. by Marybeth Bond. Traveler's Tales, 1995.

Periodicals and Organizations

- *Journeywoman*
  50 Prince Arthur Avenue, Suite 1703
  Toronto, Ont M5R 1B5
  (416) 929-7654

  Excellent quarterly networking newsletter for women travelers. Regularly features tips and tales from readers.

- Spa Finders
  91 Fifth Avenue, Suite 801
  New York, NY 10003
  (800) 255-7727

  A travel agency that specializes in matching people to spa vacations. They put out a quarterly newsletter.

- *Travelin' Woman*
  855 Moraga Drive #14
  Los Angeles, CA 90049
  (310) 472-6318

  A newsletter with travel information, tips, and advice for women.

- The Women's Travel Club
  8180 Erwin Road
  Miami, FL 33143
  (800) 480-4448

  Women-only trips to foreign and domestic destinations. Newsletter available with membership, but non-members can travel.

- *Women's Traveller*
  Damron Company
  PO Box 458
  San Francisco, CA 94142-2458
  (415) 255-0404

  Detailed directory to the US, Canada, and Caribbean for the lesbian traveler. Includes maps and overviews to major metropolitan and resort areas.

Notes

Notes

Notes